Copyright© 2024 Gail Short

All rights reserved. No portion of this book may be reproduced in any form without prior permission from the copyright owner of this book.

This book is dedicated to my grandson and all the
children who have enjoyed my first book
<u>Donuts Everywhere</u>
I love hearing the stories of you enjoying the book
and seeing pictures of you reading it.
Much Love,
Gail

THE SILLY STICKER

One morning Samantha got ready for daycare and she was wearing... her pink shirt and her blue skirt. She had fun getting ready for daycare that morning and she decided to wear a sticker on her shirt. She chose a happy face sticker. She was happy and excitedly looked forward to showing her friends her sticker.

When they arrived at daycare, Samantha said a quick goodbye to her Mom and ran over to her friends to say "good morning" and she showed them her sticker. They all chatted about their favorite stickers for a little while and then they all went off to play in the block area.

A B
C D
1 2
3

A little while later...
Samantha's sticker fell off her shirt and landed on the floor, but Samantha didn't notice that it was missing from her shirt.

A B
C D
1
2
3

Roman walked into the block area and he found the sticker on the floor. He was surprised and thought Samantha didn't want it anymore, so he happily put it on his shirt.

A B
C D
1
2
3

But a little while later...
Roman gave it to his friend Jake to help cheer him up. Jake was sad because he was missing his Mom today. Jake had it on his pants for a while and it made him happy that Roman shared it with him. Samantha saw this and it made her feel happy too.

A B
C D
1
2

But a little while later...
Jake wanted to play at the water table for a while because the teacher made green water and had droppers and sponges in there today. Jake loved counting the drops. So...
Jake put it on the shelf so that it wouldn't get wet.

Mary walked by and found it on the shelf and she
put it on her sneaker.
But a little while later...it fell off while she was in
the bathroom.

The teacher found the sticker and said "I've been
seeing this sticker all morning.
It's been everywhere.
Is this sticker silly or what?"

The teacher put the sticker on her shirt!

All the boys and girls looked at each other as they realized it was indeed a silly sticker.
But a little while later...
the sticker became even more silly.

It fell from the teacher's shirt and right into
Amy's hair.
A little while later...
it fell on the table and got in Scott's playdough.

A little while later...
it was on a chair, then on the blocks, then on the
easel.

Finally, it came back to the teacher and she put it
on the wall.

A little while later...
everyone looked but the sticker was gone.

Now no one knew where the sticker was.
Do you?

www.ingramcontent.com/pod-product-compliance
Lightning Source LLC
Chambersburg PA
CBHW042136030726
47599CB00002B/486